One Pot

igloo

igloo

Published by Igloo Books Ltd
Cottage Farm
Sywell
NN6 0BJ
www.igloo-books.com

10 9 8 7 6 5 4 3 2 1

ISBN: 978 1 84852 719 5

Project Managed by R&R Publications Marketing Pty Ltd

Food Photography: R&R Photostudio (www.rrphotostudio.com.au)
Recipe Development: R&R Test Kitchen

Front cover photograph © Stockfood/Jean Cazais

Printed in and manufactured in China

Contents

Lamb Shanks with Root Vegetables

Preparation 20 mins **Cooking** 1 hr 15 mins **Calories** 646

- 2 tbsps olive oil
- 2 parsnips, peeled and cut into large chunks
- 1 medium sweet potato, peeled, and cut into large chunks
- 1 turnip, peeled and cut into large chunks
- 1 bunch scallions, trimmed
- 2 cloves garlic, crushed
- 4 lamb shanks
- ¾ cup beef stock
- ¼ cup water
- ½ cup red wine
- 1 tbsp tomato paste
- 2 sprigs rosemary, chopped
- a bouquet garni
- freshly ground pepper and salt

1. Heat 1 tablespoon of the oil in a large heavy-based saucepan, add the root vegetables and cook quickly until brown. Set aside on a plate. Add the extra oil to the pan and brown the garlic and lamb for a few minutes.
2. To the pan, add the stock, water, red wine, tomato paste, rosemary, bouquet garni, pepper, and salt. Bring to the boil, reduce the heat, and leave to simmer, with the lid on, for 20 minutes.
3. Return the vegetables to the pan, and continue to cook for another 30 minutes, until everything is cooked.
4. Before serving, remove the bouquet garni and check the seasoning.

Serves 4

Note: You could use 1 kg (2¼ lb) osso bucco instead of the lambshanks to vary this recipe.

Lamb Korma

Preparation 10 mins **Cooking** approximately 120 mins **Calories** 615

1½ kg (3⅓lb) shoulder of lamb
salt and freshly ground black pepper
2 tbsps butter
1 red onion, finely chopped
1 clove garlic, finely chopped
1 tbsp curry paste
¼ tsp ground ginger
¼ tsp turmeric
⅛ tsp cayenne pepper
2 tbsp flour
1¼ cups chicken stock
¾ cup golden raisins
½ cup yogurt
1 tbsp lemon juice

1. Cut the lamb from the bone into 4cm cubes. Season with salt and pepper.
2. Heat the butter in a large, heavy-based saucepan, add a third of the lamb and brown well on all sides. Remove and brown the remaining lamb in 2 batches. Remove lamb from pan.
3. Add the onion and garlic and sauté until translucent. Stir in the curry paste, spices, and flour and cook for 1 minute. Add the stock, golden raisins and lamb. Cover with a lid and simmer gently for 1 hour or until the lamb is very tender, stirring occasionally.
4. Stir in the yogurt and lemon juice. Serve with boiled rice and sambals.

Serves 4–6

Lamb and Sweet Potato Stew

Preparation 25 mins **Cooking** 1 hr 50 mins **Calories** 662

- 1 tbsp olive oil
- 12 lamb chops
- 4 cups lamb or chicken stock
- 2 onions, thinly sliced
- 700g (1½lb) sweet potatoes, cut into 1cm (½in) thick slices
- 1¼ cups carrots, chopped
- 5 stalks celery, chopped
- 6–7 fresh sage leaves or 1 tsp dried sage
- 4–5 fresh thyme sprigs or 1 tsp dried thyme
- salt and black pepper
- 3 tbsps pearl barley

1 Preheat the oven to 190°C (380°F). Heat the oil in a large, heavy-based skillet and fry the chops for 1–2 minutes each side to brown (you may have to do this in batches). Remove the chops, discard the oil and add about half a cup of stock to the pan. Bring to the boil, stirring and scraping the bottom of the pan, then add to the rest of the stock.

2 Place half the onions in a large ovenproof dish. Top with ⅓ of the sweet potatoes, then add half the carrots and celery and all the sage, thyme, and chops. Season, then sprinkle with the barley. Repeat the layering and top with the remaining sweet potatoes. Pour over the stock and cover.

3 Cook for 1½ hours or until the lamb is tender, checking occasionally and adding more stock or water if the stew becomes too dry. Remove the lid and increase the oven heat to 230°C (450°F). Cook for 8–10 minutes, until the sweet potatoes have browned.

Serves 6

Note: A hearty alternative to the traditional hotpot. The fresh herbs make tender lamb cutlets and vegetables extra tasty, though the dish also works with dried herbs.

Lamb and Prune Tagine

Preparation 20 mins **Cooking** approximately 2 hrs **Calories** 100

400g (14oz) lamb cubed
1 medium onion, finely chopped
½ tsp ground ginger
1½ cups chicken stock
1 cinnamon stick
salt and pepper to taste
1 cup pitted prunes
1 tbsp honey
2 tsps grated orange rind

Note: You could use prunes instead of apricots and orange rind instead of lemon rind to vary this recipe.

1. Cut a circle of baking paper to be 4cm (1½in) larger in diameter than the base of the saucepan being used. Line the saucepan with the cut circle, pressing it well into the sides.
2. Heat the saucepan on high heat, add the lamb cubes and onion and spread in a single layer. When the underside has changed colour, toss over to sear and seal all areas, tossing at intervals. Add the ginger, stir to coat the meat, pour in half a cup of stock then immediately pull out the baking paper and set aside. Add the remaining stock, cinnamon stick, salt, and pepper. Bring to the boil, immediately reduce the heat to a simmer. Place the reserved baking paper circle to rest on top of the meat to contain the steam, and simmer for 50 minutes.
3. Remove the baking paper and discard. Stir in the prunes, honey, and orange rind. Simmer, covered, for 40 minutes or until the lamb is tender. Remove the lid to reduce the liquid content for the last 10 minutes of cooking. Serve over steamed couscous.

Serves 4

Slow-Simmered Lamb Shanks with Couscous

Preparation 15 mins **Cooking** 1 hr 40 mins **Calories** 430

- 4 Frenched lamb shanks (ask your butcher to do this)
- 2 cups canned chopped tomatoes
- 1 cup red wine
- 1 bay leaf
- 6 sprigs fresh thyme
- 1 cinnamon stick
- 1½ cups pumpkin, cut into large pieces
- 2 zucchinis, cut into large pieces
- 8 dried apricots
- 8 dried prunes
- 1 cup couscous
- 2 tbsps flaked almonds, toasted

1. Preheat the oven to 160°C (325°F). Heat a large skillet over a high heat and sear the lamb shanks in batches until browned all over. Transfer to an ovenproof casserole dish.
2. Add the tomatoes, wine, bay leaf, thyme, and cinnamon stick. Cover and bake for 1 hour. Add the pumpkin, zucchini, apricots, and prunes and cook uncovered for 30 minutes longer or until the vegetables are soft and the lamb starts to come away from the bone.
3. Put the couscous in a large bowl, cover with 2 cups of boiling water and allow it to stand for 10 minutes or until all the liquid is absorbed.
4. Serve the lambs shanks in deep bowls on top of the couscous and garnished with the flaked almonds.

Serves 4

Note: The term Frenched refers to the cutting and scraping of all meat, fat and gristle from the bone, leaving the meaty part virtually fat free.

Slow-Cooked Lamb and Macadamias

Preparation 15 mins + marinating time **Cooking** 2 hrs 15 mins **Calories** 360

- 700g (1½lb) boneless leg lamb, trimmed of visible fat, cut into 2cm cubes
- ⅓ cup raisins
- ½ cup evaporated milk

Spicy Yogurt Marinade

- 1 white onion, diced
- ⅓ cup ground unsalted macadamias
- 2cm piece fresh ginger, chopped
- ½ cup plain yoghurt
- 2 tsps lime or lemon juice
- 3 tsps ground cilantro
- 2 tsps ground cardamom
- ½ tsp freshly ground black pepper

1. To make the marinade, place the onion, macadamias, ginger, yogurt, and lime or lemon juice in a blender. Process to combine. Stir in cilantro, cardamom and pepper.
2. Place the lamb in a non-metalic dish. Pour over the marinade and toss to coat. Cover and marinate in the refrigerator overnight.
3. Transfer the meat mixture to a heavy-based saucepan. Stir in the raisins and evaporated milk. Place the pan over a medium heat and bring to a simmer. Reduce the heat to low. Cover and cook, stirring occasionally, for 1½ hours.
4. Remove cover. Cook, stirring occasionally, for 30–40 minutes longer or until meat is tender and the sauce is thick. Add a little water during cooking, if necessary.
5. Serve with boiled rice and steamed vegetables of your choice.

Serves 4

Lamb Casserole with Couscous and Gremolata

Preparation 30 mins **Cooking** 1 hr **Calories** 681

- sea salt and freshly ground black pepper
- 2 tbsps flour
- 4 cups diced lamb, trimmed of excess fat
- 2–3 tbsps extra virgin olive oil
- 1 yellow and 1 green capsicum, deseeded and chopped
- 2 cups canned chopped tomatoes

Gremolata

- 1 garlic clove, very finely chopped
- 3 tbsps fresh parsley, finely chopped
- grated rind of 1 lemon

Couscous

- 2 cups couscous
- 1 tbsp extra virgin olive oil
- 1 large onion, finely sliced

1. Preheat the oven to 180°C (350°F). Season the flour and spread it on a large plate, then toss the meat in the seasoned flour until coated. Heat the oil in a large skillet and cook the meat over a medium heat for 2–3 minutes each side, until browned (you'll need to do this in 2 batches). Transfer the browned meat to an ovenproof dish, using a slotted spoon.
2. Add the capsicums to the skillet and cook for 2 minutes. Add the tomatoes and bring to the boil. Add these to the lamb and cook in the oven for 40 minutes or until the meat is tender. Meanwhile, mix all the gremolata ingredients together.
3. Prepare the couscous according to the packet instructions, then fluff it up with a fork. Heat the oil in a small skillet and cook the onion over a medium heat for 10 minutes until golden brown. Add to the couscous and mix well. Sprinkle the gremolata over the lamb casserole and serve with the couscous.

Serves 4

Note: Gremolata is a mixture of finely chopped herbs, garlic, and citrus zest. Adding this to the casserole just before serving adds a fresh new dimension of flavor.

Lemon and Thyme Lamb

Preparation 20 mins **Cooking** approximately 1 hr 45 mins **Calories** 100

750g (1¾lb) lean diced lamb forequarter
1 tbsp olive oil
1 tbsp thyme leaves
2 tsps freshly crushed garlic
1 onion, chopped
¼ cup flour
¼ cup lemon juice
½ cup sweet white wine
¾ cup chicken stock
black pepper
1½ cups rice
6 spinach leaves, chopped
3 large carrots, julienne
sprigs fresh thyme

1. Combine lamb, oil, thyme, and garlic. Brown lamb in non-stick pan with onion. Add flour and cook for 5 minutes. Pour in lemon juice, wine, and stock.
2. Cover and simmer for 1½ hours, stirring occasionally, or cook in covered ovenproof dish at 160°C (325°F) for 1½ hours. Season with pepper.
3. Meanwhile, cook rice according to packet directions. Microwave or steam spinach for 3–4 minutes and carrots for 3–4 minutes. Combine rice and spinach.
4. Serve lamb with rice and carrots. Garnish with thyme.

Serves 4–6

Note: Diced lamb from the forequarter is best in this recipe.

Bobotie

Preparation 10 mins plus soaking time **Cooking** 1 hr **Calories** 361

- 2 kg (4½lb) boned leg or shoulder of lamb
- 4 large dried peaches, chopped
- ½ cup seeded raisins, chopped
- 1 slice white bread
- ¼ cup milk
- 2 tbsps butter or oil
- 3 large onions, finely chopped
- 2 tbsps curry powder
- 1 tbsp brown sugar
- salt and freshly ground black pepper
- ¼ cup lemon juice
- 3 eggs
- ¼ cup almonds
- 4 lemon or bay leaves
- ¾ cup milk, extra

1. Preheat oven to 160°C (325°F). Trim the fat from the lamb and grind it coarsely in a blender. Soak the dried fruit in water for 30 minutes, drain and set aside. Soak the bread in a quarter cup milk.
2. Heat the butter or oil in a large skillet, add the lamb and brown thoroughly, stirring and breaking up lumps with the back of a wooden spoon. Remove from the pan to a large bowl.
3. Add the onions and extra oil to the pan (if needed), and fry the onions until soft but not colored. Add the curry powder, sugar, salt, and pepper and stir for 1 minute. Stir in the lemon juice, dissolving brown pan juices. Bring to simmer, then pour the contents of the pan over the meat. Add the milk-soaked bread, 1 of the eggs and the peaches, raisins, and almonds. Knead by hand to combine all the ingredients well.
4. Pack the lamb into a greased ovenproof dish and smooth the top. Tuck the lemon or bay leaves under the surface of the meat.
5. Beat the 2 remaining eggs with the extra three quarters cup milk, season lightly and pour over the surface of the meat. Bake in a preheated oven for 40 minutes, until the surface is browned and firm. Serve hot with boiled rice.

Serves 6–8

Note: A terrific South African dish which mixes the taste of India with the wilds of South Africa.

Lamb and Apricot Stew

Preparation 15 mins **Cooking** 2 hrs 20 mins **Calories** 335

- 4 ripe tomatoes, blanched and peeled
- 2 tbsps oil
- 1 green capsicum, seeded and finely chopped
- 1 large onion, chopped
- 2 tbsps fresh mint, chopped
- 6 cups lamb cubes, cut from the leg or shoulder
- ⅔ cup dried apricots
- salt and freshly ground black pepper

1. Cut the tomatoes in half crosswise (through the 'equator'), gently squeeze out the seeds and chop the tomatoes.
2. Heat ½ the oil in a heavy-based, lidded skillet or saucepan, add the tomatoes, capsicum, onion and mint and for the sauté for 5 minutes. Remove from the pan.
3. Heat the remaining oil, add the lamb and stir it quickly to brown on all sides. Return the vegetables to the pan, add the apricots and enough water to almost cover the meat. Bring to the boil, turn down the heat, and simmer for 1 hour.
4. After the hour season with salt and pepper. Check the liquid content and add more water if needed. Simmer for 1 hour more, until the lamb is very tender. Serve with boiled rice.

Serves 6

Mediterranean Beef and Olive Casserole

Preparation 30 mins + 4 hrs marinating **Cooking** 3 hrs 15 mins **Calories** 474

grated zest and juice of 1 lemon

1⅓ kg (3lb) lean braising steak, cut into 5cm chunks

2 tbsps olive oil

3 tbsps drained pitted black olives, plus 15 to serve

4 tomatoes, quartered and deseeded

salt and black pepper

chopped fresh parsley to garnish

Marinade

2 medium onions, chopped

2 cloves garlic, crushed

3 bay leaves

3 fresh thyme sprigs or 2 tsps dried thyme

1 tsp dried oregano

2 tbsps chopped fresh parsley

1 small bulb fennel, chopped

2 carrots, sliced

8 black peppercorns

2 tbsps olive oil

1 bottle dry white wine

1 Fill a large non-metallic bowl with cold water and add the lemon juice. Rinse the meat in the lemon water then drain well. Mix together all the marinade ingredients, then add the meat and coat. Cover and refrigerate for 4 hours or overnight.

2 Preheat the oven to 160°C (325°F). Lift the meat out of the bowl, reserving the marinade, and drain well. Coat a large, flame and ovenproof dish with 1 tablespoon of the oil. Add half the meat and fry for 6–7 minutes, until browned, turning once. Set aside, then fry the remaining meat. Stir in the marinade and the pitted olives and mix well.

3 Cover the dish with a double layer of aluminum foil, then a lid. Cook for 2 hours. Remove the lid and aluminum foil, press the meat down with the back of a wooden spoon and top with the tomatoes. Season lightly and drizzle over the remaining oil. Cover the dish with the aluminum foil and lid again and cook for 1 hour or until the beef is tender.

4 Skim off any surface fat. Season if necessary, then sprinkle over the lemon zest, parsley, and the remaining olives. Serve from the dish.

Serves 6

Jarkoy

Preparation 20 mins **Cooking** 2 hrs 30 mins **Calories** 449

- 1 kg (2¼lb) thick-cut beefsteak
- 2 tbsps butter or oil
- 3 large carrots, thinly sliced
- 3 medium onions, thinly sliced
- 2 tbsps flour
- 2 cloves garlic, crushed
- 1 tsp chopped fresh dill or ½ tsp dried dill
- ½ tsp nutmeg, grated or ground
- salt and freshly ground black pepper
- 1½ cups rich beef stock
- ½ cup dried apricots
- ½ cup dried peaches, quartered
- ½ cup pitted prunes
- 1 tsp chopped mint
- 1 tbsp chopped cilantro
- ½ cup walnuts, crushed
- ¼ cup orange juice

1. Trim the fat from the steak and cut it into large cubes. Heat a large heavy-based saucepan, add the butter or oil, and ⅓ of the beef cubes. Toss to brown well on all sides over a high heat. Remove and brown the remainder in 2 batches. Add the carrots and onions and sauté a little.
2. Return all the meat to the saucepan and sprinkle in the flour to cover all the surface. Add the garlic, dill, nutmeg, salt, pepper, and stock. Bring to the boil over a high heat, stirring to lift the browned-on juices. Cover, reduce the heat to low and simmer slowly for 1½ hours.
3. Add the dried fruits, prunes, mint, and cilantro. Cover and simmer 30 minutes more, or until the meat is tender. Remove to a heated serving dish. Sprinkle with the walnuts and orange juice.

Serves 6

Beef Carbonade

Preparation 15 mins **Cooking** 2 hrs 30 mins **Calories** 506

- 2–3 tbsps vegetable oil
- 1 kg (2¼lb) braising or stewing steak, cut into 2cm cubes
- 1 large onion, thinly sliced
- 1 tbsp flour
- 2 tbsps soft dark brown sugar
- 1 can Guinness stout
- 2 cups beef stock
- 1 tbsp tomato paste
- 1 bouquet garni
- salt and black pepper
- fresh parsley to garnish

1 Preheat the oven to 160°C (325°F). Heat 2 tablespoons of the oil in an ovenproof dish. Add a third of the beef and fry over a high heat for 6–7 minutes, turning until browned on all sides. Remove from the pan while you cook the remaining batches, adding more oil if necessary. Set the beef aside.

2 Lower the heat, add the onion and cook for 5 minutes, stirring. Sprinkle in the flour and sugar and stir for 1–2 minutes, then pour in the Guinness and stock and bring to the boil, stirring. Return the beef to the dish and add the tomato paste and bouquet garni. Season and stir well, then cover.

3 Transfer the dish to the oven and cook for 1½–2 hours, until the beef is tender and cooked through. Stir 2–3 times during cooking, adding a little water if necessary. Discard the bouquet garni and season again if necessary. Garnish with the parsley.

Serves 4

Note: Almost everyone loves a good old-fashioned stew, and you can't beat a beef one. Serve with plenty of creamy mashed potatoes to soak up the rich gravy.

Steak and Kidney Puffs

Preparation 20 mins **Cooking** 2 hrs 50 mins **Calories** 650

- 2–4 tbsps groundnut oil
- 1 onion, finely chopped
- 500g (18oz) braising steak, trimmed of excess fat and cubed
- 350g (12oz) pig's kidney, halved, cores removed, then cut into 1cm pieces
- 3 tbsps plain flour
- 1 tbsp tomato paste
- 2 tsps Worcestershire sauce
- 1½ cups beef stock
- finely grated zest of 1 lemon
- 2 tbsps finely chopped fresh parsley, plus extra to garnish
- 1 tsp dried mixed herbs
- salt and black pepper
- ½ cup baby button mushrooms
- 1 pack ready-rolled puff pastry
- fresh rosemary to garnish

1. Preheat the oven to 160°C (325°F). Heat 2 tablespoons of the oil in a large ovenproof and flameproof dish, add the onion and cook for 5 minutes. Add ½ the steak and kidney and fry over a high heat, stirring, for 6 minutes or until browned. Keep warm. Fry the remaining meat, adding more oil if necessary.
2. Return all the meat to the dish, add the flour and stir for 2 minutes. Add the tomato paste, Worcestershire sauce, stock, lemon zest, parsley, herbs, salt, and pepper. Bring to boil, stirring, then cover.
3. Transfer to the oven. After 1½ hours, stir in the mushrooms and a little water, if needed. Cook for 35 minutes more. Meanwhile, unroll the pastry and cut it into 4 x 11cm (4in) circles. Put them on a baking sheet.
4. Take the dish out of the oven. Increase the oven temperature to 200°C (400°F). Meanwhile, place the dish over a very low heat. Keep covered but stir occasionally. Bake the pastry for 20 minutes or until golden brown. Top each pastry circle with the steak and kidney. Garnish with the chopped parsley and rosemary and serve.

Serves 4

Note: You could use 2 cups of sliced field mushrooms instead of kidneys to vary this recipe.

Steak Pie with Guinness

Preparation 30 mins **Cooking** 3 hrs **Calories** 628

- 3 tbsps flour
- 1 tsp English mustard powder
- salt and black pepper
- 1 kg (2¼lb) stewing beef, cubed
- 4 tbsps vegetable oil
- 2 onions, sliced
- 2 cloves garlic, finely chopped
- 2 cups Guinness stout
- 2 tbsps Worcestershire sauce
- 2 bay leaves
- 1 tbsp chopped fresh thyme
- 1 tsp soft dark brown sugar
- 1 cup chestnut mushrooms, halved if large

Pastry Crust

- 2 cups flour
- ½ tsp baking powder
- 2 tsps chopped fresh thyme
- salt and freshly ground black pepper
- ½ cup cold butter,grated

1 Preheat the oven to 160°C (325°F). Combine the flour, mustard and pepper, then coat the beef in the mixture. Heat 2 tablespoons of the oil in a heavy-based skillet. Fry a third of the beef for 3–4 minutes, until browned. Transfer to an ovenproof dish and fry the rest of the beef in 2 more batches.

2 Add tablespoon of oil to the pan, then fry the onions for 5 minutes. Add the garlic and cook for 2 minutes. Stir in the Guinness, Worcestershire sauce, bay leaves, thyme, and sugar and simmer for 2–3 minutes. Pour over the beef, then cover and cook in the oven for 2 hours. Remove the dish and increase the oven temperature to 190°C (380°F). Fry the mushrooms in the rest of the oil. Stir into the beef, then transfer to a 15 x 20cm (6x8in) pie dish.

3 To make the pastry crust, sift together the flour, baking powder and half teaspoon of the salt, then add the thyme and pepper to taste. Stir in the butter and bind with 10–12 tablespoons of water to form a soft dough. Roll it out, dampen the edges of the dish and cover it with the pastry. Trim, then make a small slit in the centre. Cook for 30–40 minutes, until golden.

Serves 6

Note: Guinness adds its creamy richness to this slow-cooked steak pie. Serve with mash and peas or cabbage.

Belgian Beef Casserole

Preparation 10 mins **Cooking** 2 hrs 40 mins **Calories** 329

- 700g (1½lb) stewing beef, cubed
- 2 tbsps dripping or other fat
- 2 onions, sliced
- 1 tbsp flour
- 1 cup beer
- 1 cup hot beef stock
- 1 clove garlic, crushed
- 1 bouquet garni
- salt and freshly ground black pepper
- ½ tsp nutmeg
- ½ tsp sugar
- 1 tsp vinegar
- 8 slices French bread, 2cm (1in) thick
- French mustard

1 Preheat the oven to 160°C (325°F). Brown the meat in the hot dripping in a flameproof, ovenproof dish, then lower the heat and add the onions. Cook for 2 minutes. Sprinkle with the flour, pour over beer and stock and stir until boiling. Add the garlic, bouquet garni, salt, pepper, nutmeg, sugar, and vinegar. Cover and cook in a moderately slow oven for 2 hours or until the meat is tender.

2 Remove the dish from the oven and remove the bouquet garni. Skim off the fat and spoon it over the bread slices, then spread the bread thickly with mustard. Arrange the bread on top of the beef, pushing well into gravy (it will float to the top). Cook, uncovered, for a further 30 minutes or until the bread forms a good brown crust.

Serves 4–6

Slowly Simmered Indonesian Beef Curry

Preparation 25 mins **Cooking** 3 hrs 15 mins **Calories** 462

- 2 stalks lemongrass
- 4 tbsps dried coconut
- 2 onions, chopped
- 2 cloves garlic, crushed
- 5cm fresh root ginger, chopped
- 1 red chili, deseeded and chopped, plus 1 red chili, deseeded and sliced, to garnish
- 2 tbsps vegetable oil
- 700g (1½lb) beef steak, cut into 2cm cubes
- 1 tsp turmeric
- 1½ cups canned coconut milk
- 1 tsp sugar
- salt

1 Peel the outer layers from the lemongrass stalks, then finely chop the lower white bulbous parts, discarding the fibrous tops. Heat a large saucepan and dry-fry the coconut for 5 minutes or until golden, stirring frequently. Finely grind the coconut in a blender or with a pestle and mortar.

2 Blend or grind to a paste the lemongrass, onions, garlic, ginger, and chili. Heat the oil in the pan and fry the paste for 5 minutes to release the flavors, stirring often. Add the beef, stir to coat and fry for 3–4 minutes, until sealed.

3 Add the ground coconut, turmeric, coconut milk, sugar, and salt to taste, and mix well. Bring to the boil, stirring, then reduce the heat. Simmer, uncovered, for 3 hours, stirring from time to time, until the sauce reduces to a rich gravy. Garnish with the sliced chili and serve with rice.

Serves 4

Note: Rendang, a classic Indonesian dish, can also be made with lamb or venison. Slow cooking in the rich coconut sauce results in meltingly tender meat.

Beef Braised in Rioja

Preparation 20 mins **Cooking** 2 hrs 15 mins **Calories** 487

- 3 tbsps olive oil
- 700g (1½lb) stewing beef, trimmed of fat and cut into 6cm (2in) chunks
- 6 shallots, finely chopped
- 2 garlic cloves, crushed
- 2 stalks celery, thickly sliced
- 1½ cups mushrooms, thickly sliced
- ½ tsp ground allspice
- ½ bottle Rioja, or full-bodied red wine
- 1 cup tomato purée
- 2 sprigs fresh thyme
- salt and freshly ground black pepper

1 Preheat the oven to 180°C (350°F). Heat the oil in a flameproof, ovenproof dish or a large saucepan and fry the meat over a high heat, stirring, for 5–10 minutes, until browned. Remove from the pan, then add the shallots, garlic, and celery. Cook, stirring, for 3–4 minutes, until lightly browned.

2 Add the mushrooms and cook for 1 minute or until softened. Stir in the allspice, wine, tomato purée, 1 sprig of thyme, and seasoning. Return the meat to the dish or pan and bring the mixture to a simmer.

3 Cover and cook in the oven or over a low heat on the hob for 1½–2 hours, until the beef is tender. Season again if necessary, then serve garnished with the remaining thyme.

Serves 4

Note: This Spanish dish is perfect on a cold day served with garlic mash. You can use any type of mushroom, but ceps or chestnut mushrooms are especially good.

Rich Beef Stew with Shallots

Preparation 20 mins **Cooking** 3 hrs 10 mins **Calories** 471

6 shallots, quartered
6 large cloves garlic, quartered
3 large carrots, sliced
4 stalks celery, sliced
4 tbsps olive oil
1¼ kg (2¾lb) lean stewing beef, cut into 5cm (2in) cubes
a few thyme sprigs, 1 bay leaf, 1 rosemary sprig and 1 strip of lemon zest, tied with string
2 cups full-bodied red wine
1 cup beef stock
3 tbsps pearled barley
10 black peppercorns, crushed
salt and black pepper

1. Preheat the oven to 240°C (460°F). Place the shallots, garlic, carrots, and celery in a roasting tin, pour over 2 tablespoons of oil, and mix well. Cook for 15 minutes, turning frequently, or until the vegetables are browned.
2. Heat the remaining oil in a large, heavy-based saucepan. Add a third of the meat and fry for 5–8 minutes, until browned all over. Remove from the pan and set aside while you cook the remaining meat in 2 more batches. Return all the meat to the saucepan. Add the vegetables, herb bundle, wine, stock, barley, and peppercorns. Season and bring to the boil.
3. Reduce the heat and simmer, partly covered, for 2–2½ hours, until the meat is tender. Check from time to time and add a little more stock or water if the stew starts to dry out. Remove the herb bundle before serving.

Serves 6

Note: There are times when all you want is a warming stew, especially if the weather's bad. Serve with comforting mashed potato with chopped fresh parsley stirred in.

Venison Casserole with Chilli Beans

Preparation 20 mins **Cooking** 2 hrs 30 mins **Calories** 427

- 2 tbsps plain flour
- salt and black pepper
- 700g (1½lb) diced shoulder of venison
- 2 tbsps groundnut oil
- 1 red onion, finely chopped
- 2 cloves garlic, crushed
- 2 fresh green chilies, deseeded and finely chopped
- 1 tbsp chili powder
- 2 cups canned chopped tomatoes
- 2 cups beef stock
- 2 tbsps tomato paste
- 2 tsps soft light or dark brown sugar
- 2 cups canned kidney beans, drained and rinsed

1 Preheat the oven to 150°C (300°F). Mix the flour, salt, and pepper together on a plate. Dip the venison into the mixture to coat. Heat the oil in a large flameproof, ovenproof dish and fry the venison in batches over a medium to high heat for 5 minutes, or until browned on all sides. Remove from the dish and set aside.

2 Lower the heat and add the onion to the dish with a little more oil, if necessary. Stir for 5 minutes or until lightly browned, then add the garlic, chilies and chili powder and stir for, 1 minute.

3 Add the tomatoes, stock, tomato paste, and sugar. Bring to the boil, stirring. Add the venison, stir well and cover tightly with the lid. Transfer the dish to the oven and cook for 2 hours or until the venison is tender, stirring twice and adding the beans for the last 30 minutes of cooking.

Serves 4

Note: You could use chickpeas instead of kidney beans to vary this recipe.

Normandy Chicken

Preparation 20 mins **Cooking** approximately 1 hr **Calories** 127

- 1 kg (2¼lb) chicken thigh pieces
- ¼ cup flour
- ¼ tsp nutmeg, grated
- salt and black pepper
- 1½ tbsps oil
- 3 green apples
- 1 onion, finely chopped
- 2 tbsps cider vinegar
- 1 cup cider
- ½ cup sour cream
- 2 tsps cornstarch

1. Preheat the oven to 200°C (400°F). Wash thighs, trim remove skin, and pat dry. Mix flour, nutmeg, salt and pepper together. Roll thigh pieces in flour and shake off excess. Heat oil in a frying pan and brown the thigh pieces on both sides. Transfer thighs to an ovenproof dish.

2. Slice apples into rings and remove core. Fry them on both sides in the frying pan and place over the chicken in the dish. Fry the onion and place in the dish. Drain the oil from the pan, add cider vinegar and cider, heat to lift pan juices and then pour over the chicken. Cover the dish, cook in the oven for 40 minutes.

3. Remove chicken and apples to a serving platter, cover and keep hot. Skim fat from remaining juices and pour juices into a saucepan. Stir in the sour cream and blended cornstarch, stir over gentle heat until sauce thickens, then pour over chicken.

Serves 6

Chicken Cacciatore

Preparation 15 mins **Cooking** approximately 1 hr **Calories** 130

- 1 kg (2¼lb) chicken breasts
- 4 tbsps seasoned flour
- 4 tbsps olive oil
- 1 green capsicum, diced
- 1 medium onion, finely chopped
- 2 cloves garlic, crushed
- 425g (15oz) canned tomatoes
- 1 tbsp tomato paste
- 1 bay leaf
- 1 tsp oregano
- 1 tsp sugar
- ¼ cup dry white wine
- ¼ cup marsala
- 10 black olives
- 2 tbsps chopped parsley

1 Cut each breast through the bone into 2 or 3 pieces. Coat well with seasoned flour (flour mixed with salt and pepper).

2 Heat oil to hot in a heavy wide-based saucepan and fry chicken a few pieces at a time until golden brown on all sides. Remove to aplate. Drain oil from the pan leaving about 1 tablespoon.

3 Add capsicum, onion, and garlic and sauté for 3 minutes. Chop the tomatoes and add with their juice; add tomato paste, bay leaf, oregano, and sugar. Bring to the boil, allow to simmer for 5 minutes. Return chicken to the pan, add wine and marsala, cover and simmer slowly for 35 minutes.

4 Transfer to serving platter, sprinkle with black olives and parsley and serve.

Serves 4–6

Kashmir Pork Curry

Preparation 10 mins + 15 mins standing **Cooking** approximately 2 hrs **Calories** 130

- 750g (1¾lb) lean diced pork
- 1 tsp sugar
- 1 tsp ground turmeric
- 1 tbsp soy sauce
- 1 stem lemongrass
- 1 large onion
- 1 tbsp vegetable oil
- 4 tsps freshly chopped garlic
- 1 tbsp freshly chopped ginger
- 3 tsps freshly chopped chilies
- 1 cup water
- 425g (15oz) canned tomatoes
- 2 tsps fish sauce (optional)

1. Combine pork, sugar, and turmeric in a bowl. Add soy sauce and let stand for 15 minutes.
2. Thinly slice approximately 7cm of lemongrass stem. Cut onion into large pieces.
3. Heat oil, lightly sauté lemongrass, onion, garlic, ginger, and chili, add pork and turn constantly to brown pork.
4. Add water and tomatoes, cover and simmer for 1½–2 hours or until pork is tender. Stir occasionally.
5. Add fish sauce and serve with rice.

Serves 4–6

Note: You could use diced chicken instead of pork to vary this recipe

Chicken Curry with Jasmine Rice

Preparation 15 mins **Cooking** 40 mins **Calories** 597

- 2 cups coconut milk
- 1 cup chicken stock
- 2–3 tbsps green curry paste
- 3 kaffir lime leaves, finely shredded
- 1½ cups pumpkin, peeled and chopped
- 4 skinless chicken breast fillets, cut into small cubes
- small canned bamboo shoots, drained
- 1 cup snap beans, chopped
- 1 cup broccoli, cut into florets
- 1 tbsp fish sauce
- 1 tbsp brown sugar, grated
- 2 tbsps Thai basil leaves, torn

Jasmine Rice

- 1½ cups jasmine rice
- 2 stalks lemongrass, halved

1 Put the coconut milk, stock, curry paste, and lime leaves in wok or large pot and bring to the boil. Cook over a high heat until the sauce starts to thicken slightly. Add the pumpkin and simmer for 10 minutes, or until it starts to soften.

2 Add the chicken and bamboo shoots, reduce the heat and simmer for 10 minutes, or until the chicken is tender. Add the beans, broccoli, fish sauce, and brown sugar and cook, uncovered, until the vegetables are soft.

3 Remove from the heat and stir through half the basil leaves.

4 To make the jasmine rice, put the rice, lemongrass, and 4 cups of water in a pot, bring to boil and cook over a high heat until steam holes appear in the top of the rice. Reduce the heat to low, cover and cook for 10 minutes, or until all the liquid is absorbed and the rice is tender. Transfer the rice to bowls, spoon over the curry and scatter with the remaining basil leaves.

Serves 4

Spanish Chicken with Chorizo

Preparation 15 mins **Cooking** 55 mins **Calories** 443

- 8 chicken joints, such as thighs and drumsticks
- 2 tbsps olive oil
- 1 onion, sliced
- 2 cloves garlic, crushed
- 1 red and 1 yellow capsicum, deseeded and sliced
- 2 tsps paprika
- 3 tbsps cup dry sherry or dry vermouth
- 2 cups canned chopped tomatoes
- 1 bay leaf
- 1 strip orange zest, pared with a vegetable peeler
- 1 cup chorizo, sliced
- ⅓ cup pitted black olives
- salt and black pepper

1. Place the chicken in a large non-stick skillet and fry without oil for 5–8 minutes, turning occasionally, until golden. Remove the chicken and set aside, then pour away any fat from the pan.
2. Add the oil to the pan and fry the onion, garlic, and capsicums for 3–4 minutes, until softened. Return the chicken to the pan with the paprika, sherry or vermouth, tomatoes, bay leaf, and orange zest. Bring to the boil, then simmer, covered, over a low heat for 35–40 minutes, stirring occasionally, until the chicken is cooked through.
3. Add the chorizo and olives and simmer for a further 5 minutes to heat through, then season.

Serves 4

Note: Packed with Mediterranean flavours, this dish is equally good with rice or crusty bread. You can use stock or orange juice instead of the sherry or vermouth.

Cashew Butter Chicken

Preparation 10 mins **Cooking** 1 hr **Calories** 451

- 4 tbsps butter
- 2 cloves garlic, crushed
- 2 onions, minced
- 1 tbsp curry paste
- 1 tbsp ground cilantro
- ½ tsp ground nutmeg
- 700g (1½lb) boneless chicken thigh or breast fillets, cut into 2cm cubes
- ¼ cup cashews, roasted and ground
- 1¼ cups heavy cream
- 2 tbsps coconut milk

1. Preheat oven to 180°C (350°F). To roast the cashews, spread them over a baking tray and bake for 5–10 minutes, or until lightly and evenly browned. Toss back and forth occasionally with a spoon to ensure even browning. Alternatively, place them under a medium broiler and cook, tossing back and forth, until roasted.

2. Melt the butter in a saucepan over a medium heat, add the garlic and onions and cook, stirring, for 3 minutes or until the onions are golden.

3. Stir in the curry paste, cilantro and nutmeg and cook for 2 minutes or until fragrant. Add the chicken and cook, stirring, for 5 minutes or until the chicken is brown.

4. Add the cashews, cream, and coconut milk, bring to simmering and cook, stirring occasionally, for 40 minutes or until the chicken is tender. Serve with rice.

Serves 6

Chicken Gumbo

Preparation 6 mins **Cooking** approximately 1 hr **Calories** 328

6 tbsps butter
6–8 chicken thighs, legs or wings
500g (18oz) okra
1 large onion, finely chopped
1 clove garlic, crushed
250g (9oz) ham, cut in 1 thick slice, then cubed
1 red capsicum, seeded and cubed
1½ cups peeled and chopped tomatoes
1 tbsp tomato paste
½ cup dry white wine or chicken stock
1 bay leaf
salt and freshly ground pepper
cayenne pepper or Tabasco sauce
2 tbsps chopped parsley

1. Melt the butter in a deep skillet, add the chicken and brown on all sides. Remove and keep warm. Add the okra, onion, garlic, ham, and capsicum to the pan and stir-fry until the onion is soft.
2. Next, add the tomatoes, tomato paste, wine or stock, bay leaf, salt, pepper, and cayenne or Tabasco to taste.
3. Add the chicken to the pan, cover and simmer for 40 minutes, until the chicken is tender. Scatter with the parsley and serve with boiled rice.

Serves 4

Lovely Legs and Vegetable Casserole

Preparation 5 mins **Cooking** 55 mins **Calories** 512

340g (12oz) jar tomato and pesto sauce or packaged pesto sauce of choice

½ cup water

1 kg (2¼lb) chicken drumsticks

4 medium potatoes, peeled and quartered

2 tbsps olive oil

2 tbsps finely chopped parsley

1½ cups frozen peas

1½ cups canned baby corn

1 Preheat the oven to 180°C (350°F). Pour the tomato and pesto sauce into an ovenproof dish and stir in the water. Place the chicken in 1 layer and arrange the potato quarters in between. Drizzle over the olive oil and sprinkle with the parsley. Cover with the lid or aluminum foil.

2 Place the dish in the oven and cook for 30 minutes. Lift from oven and turn the chicken and potatoes. Add the peas and baby corn. Return to the oven and cook uncovered for 25 minutes more or until the chicken and potatoes are tender when tested.

3 Serve hot with crusty bread.

Serves 4–6

Coq au Vin

Preparation 5 mins **Cooking** 1 hr 50 mins **Calories** 677

- 2 kg (4½lb) chicken pieces
- ½ cup seasoned flour
- 2 tbsps olive oil
- 2 cloves garlic, crushed
- 12 pickling onions or shallots, peeled
- 8 slices bacon, chopped
- 1 cup chicken stock
- 3 cups red wine
- 1½ cups button mushrooms
- freshly ground black pepper

1. Toss the chicken in flour to coat. Shake off the excess flour and set aside.
2. Heat the oil in a large, non-stick skillet over a medium heat and cook the chicken in batches, turning frequently, for 10 minutes or until brown on all sides. Remove the chicken from the pan and drain on absorbent kitchen paper.
3. Add the garlic, onions or shallots, and bacon to the pan and cook, stirring, for 5 minutes or until the onions are golden. Return the chicken to the pan, stir in the stock and wine and bring to the boil. Reduce the heat, cover and simmer, stirring occasionally, for 1¼ hours or until the chicken is tender. Add the mushrooms and pepper to taste and cook for 10 minutes longer.

Serves 6

Rabbit, Olive and Onion Casserole

Preparation 5 mins + marinating time **Cooking** 1 hr 30 mins **Calories** 458

- 700g (1½lb) rabbit portions
- 2 cups dry white wine
- 3 sprigs fresh oregano
- 3 bay leaves
- 5 tbsps olive oil
- 1 cup baby onions, peeled and halved
- 6 cloves garlic, unpeeled
- 1 tbsp paprika
- ⅔ cup chicken stock
- ½ cup black olives
- salt and freshly ground black pepper
- fresh oregano sprigs, to garnish

1 In a large bowl, combine the rabbit, wine, oregano and bay leaves. Cover and refrigerate overnight.

2 Drain the rabbit and reserve the marinade. Preheat the oven to 180°C (350°F).

3 Heat the oil in a large skillet and brown the rabbit, a few pieces at a time, on both sides. Remove the rabbit and place it in an ovenproof dish.

4 Brown the onions and garlic in the pan. Once they are golden, add the paprika. Stir continuously for 2 minutes, then add the stock and reserved marinade. Bring to the boil.

5 Pour the onion and stock mixture over the rabbit, add the olives and season with salt and pepper.

6 Cover and bake for 1 hour and 15 minutes or until the rabbit is cooked and tender. Garnish with fresh oregano sprigs and serve with plenty of the bread to mop up the juices.

Serves 4

Braised Rabbit with Dried Fruits

Preparation 5 mins **Cooking** 1 hr 20 mins **Calories** 513

- 1⅓ kg (3lb) rabbit
- salt and pepper
- 2 tbsps oil or clarified butter
- 6 small onions, halved
- 2 cups water
- 1 tbsp chopped, fresh thyme
- 2 bay leaves
- 1½ cups dried mixed fruit
- 1¼ cups red wine
- ½ cup cream

1 Wash the rabbit and pat dry. Cut into serving pieces and season with the salt and pepper. Heat the oil or butter in a large, lidded skillet or saucepan. Add the rabbit pieces and quickly brown all sides on a high heat.

2 Remove to a plate. Reduce the heat, add the onions and cook until golden. Add the water and stir to lift the pan juices. Return the rabbit to the pan, sprinkle in the chopped thyme and add the bay leaves. Cover and simmer for 40 minutes.

3 Add the dried fruit and wine, cover, and continue to simmer for 30 minutes more, or until the rabbit is tender. Add more liquid to the saucepan during cooking if necessary. Taste and adjust the seasoning. Uncover and stir in the cream. Simmer with lid off for 5 minutes. Serve with rice or mashed potato.

Serves 6

Pork Braised in Milk

Preparation 5 mins **Cooking** 2 hrs 10 mins **Calories** 406

2 tbsps butter
1 tbsp vegetable oil
1 kg (2¼lb) boneless loin pork, rolled and tied
2 cups milk
freshly ground black pepper
3 tbsps warm water

1 Heat the butter and oil in a large saucepan. When the butter is foaming, add the pork and brown on all sides.

2 Add the milk and pepper to taste and bring to the boil. Reduce the heat to low, cover and cook for 1½–2 hours or until the pork is cooked. Brush the pork occasionally with milk during cooking.

3 At end of the cooking time, the milk should have coagulated and browned in the bottom of the pan. If this has not occurred, remove the lid, and bring the liquid to the boil and boil until brown.

4 Remove the meat from the pan and set aside to cool slightly. Remove the string from the pork, cut it into slices and arrange on a serving platter. Set aside and keep warm.

5 Remove any fat from the pan, stir in the water, and bring to the boil, scraping residue from the base of the pan. Strain and spoon the pan juices over the pork to serve.

Serves 4

Apple Pork Casserole

Preparation 10 mins **Cooking** 1 hr 25 mins **Calories** 422

2 tbsps butter
2 onions, chopped
500g (18oz) lean diced pork
3 large crisp apples, peeled, cored and chopped
1 tbsp dried mixed herbs
3 cups chicken stock
freshly ground black pepper

Apple Sauce
1 tbsp butter
2 crisp apples, peeled, cored, and chopped
2 tbsps snipped fresh chives
2 cups canned tomatoes, undrained and mashed
1 tsp cracked black peppercorns

1 Heat the butter in a large skillet and cook the onions and pork over a medium heat for 5 minutes. Add the apples, herbs, stock and pepper to taste, bring to the boil, then reduce the heat and simmer for 1 hour or until the pork is tender. Using a slotted spoon, remove the pork and set aside.

2 Push the liquid and solids through a sieve and return to the pan with the pork.

3 To make the sauce, melt the butter in a skillet and cook the apples over medium heat for 2 minutes. Stir in the chives and tomatoes and bring to the boil. Reduce the heat and simmer for 5 minutes. Pour into the pan with the pork and cook over a medium heat for 5 minutes longer. Just prior to serving, sprinkle with the peppercorns.

Serves 4

Note: You could use pears instead of apples to vary this recipe

Pork in Walnut Sauce

Preparation 25 mins + 1 hr standing **Cooking** 1 hr 40 mins **Calories** 120

- 1½kg (2¼lb) lean pork
- coarse salt
- 1 tbsp butter
- freshly grated nutmeg
- freshly ground black pepper
- 1 tbsp brandy
- 4 cups milk
- 145g (5oz) shelled walnuts

1 Sprinkle pork with salt and leave for 1 hour. Preheat the oven to 200°C (400°F).

2 Rub meat with butter, and season with nutmeg and pepper. Brown on all sides in a pan, then flame with the brandy. Place meat on a low rack (or upturned plate) in a fairly deep dish that will hold meat snugly. Cover with milk and cook in the oven for 1½ hours. (You can also cook it on top of the stove over a low flame if you prefer.) After about 1 hour add the walnuts. Adjust the seasoning. You can add more milk if necessary.

3 When meat is cooked, remove it, slice it and serve the sauce separately. Mashed potato is the best accompaniment. Baked apple slices also go well. Just slice apples and bake them with a little butter, salt, a few drops of lemon juice and a pinch of cinnamon.

Serves 6

Hearty Bean Casserole

Preparation 15 mins & soaking overnight **Cooking** 1 hr 50 mins **Calories** 372

- 150g (5oz) dried kidney beans
- 150g (50z) dried black-eyed beans
- 1 tbsp vegetable oil
- 2 cloves garlic, crushed
- 1 red onion, chopped
- 440g (1lb) canned peeled tomatoes, undrained and mashed
- 1 tbsp ground cumin
- 1 tbsp dry mustard
- 2 tbsps corn syrup
- 1 tbsp tomato paste
- 2 carrots, diced
- 3 zucchini, diced
- 440g (1lb) canned butter beans, rinsed and drained
- 100g (4oz) shelled fresh or frozen broad beans
- 2 tbsps chopped fresh oregano

1 Place kidney and black-eyed beans in a large bowl, cover with water and set aside to soak overnight. Drain. Bring a large saucepan of water to the boil, add beans and boil for 10 minutes. Reduce heat and simmer for 1 hour or until beans are tender. Drain and set aside.

2 Heat oil in a large saucepan over a medium heat, add garlic and onion and cook, stirring, for 3 minutes or until onion is soft and golden. Add tomatoes, cumin, mustard, corn syrup and tomato paste and bring to the boil. Reduce heat and simmer for 5 minutes.

3 Add cooked beans, carrots, zucchini, butter beans, broad beans and oregano to pan and simmer for 30 minutes or until vegetables are tender.

Serves 4

Rich Bean and Vegetable Stew

Preparation 20 mins + 20 mins soaking **Cooking** 40 mins **Calories** 456

- ½ cup dried porcini mushrooms
- 3 tbsps olive oil
- 1½ cups large open mushrooms, chopped
- 2 carrots, finely diced
- 1 large potato, diced
- 1 cup fine green beans, chopped
- ½ tbsp dried thyme
- ½ tbsp dried sage
- 2 cloves garlic, crushed
- 1½ cups red wine
- 2 cups vegetable stock
- salt and black pepper
- 1 cup frozen fava beans
- 1 cup canned cannellini beans
- 1 cup canned flageolet beans

1. Cover the porcini mushrooms with 2½ cups of boiling water, then soak for 20 minutes. Meanwhile, heat the oil in a large saucepan and add the fresh mushrooms, carrots, potato and green beans and gently fry for 3–4 minutes, until slightly softened.
2. Add the thyme, sage, garlic, the porcini with their soaking liquid and the wine, stock and seasoning. Bring to the boil, then simmer, uncovered, for 20 minutes or until the vegetables are tender.
3. Stir in the fava beans and simmer for a further 10 minutes or until tender. Drain and rinse the cannellini and flageolet beans, add them to the mixture, then simmer for 2–3 minutes to heat through.

Serves 4

Note: This satisfying winter dish is perfect with a hunk of crusty bread to mop up the rich-red wine sauce. Serve it with a bottle of Cabernet Sauvignon.

Tuna Macaroni Casserole

Preparation 10 mins **Cooking** 45 mins **Calories** 647

- 250g (9oz) macaroni
- 2 tablespoons butter
- 2 tablespoons flour
- 1 teaspoon salt
- 1 cup milk
- 1 cup shredded aged Cheddar cheese
- 170g (6oz) canned tuna, drained
- 400g (14oz) frozen green peas
- ½ cup shredded Cheddar cheese, extra
- ¼ cup shredded Parmesan cheese

1. Preheat the oven to 175°C (340°F).
2. In a large pot of salted water boil the macaroni until tender but still firm to the bite. Drain well.
3. In a medium saucepan combine the butter, flour and salt. Stir until the butter is melted and ingredients are combined evenly.
4. Add the milk and beat until the white sauce thickens (usually it is at the proper consistency by the time it begins to boil). Add the cheese to the mixture and beat until the cheese is melted and mixture is well blended.
5. Stir in the tuna and peas.
6. In a casserole dish combine the macaroni and tuna mixture. Sprinkle extra Cheddar and Parmesan cheese on top and bake for 30 minutes until the top is golden.

Serves 4

Manhattan Oyster Chowder

Preparation 25 mins **Cooking** approximately 1 hr **Calories** 45

- 2 tbsps olive oil
- 1 onion, chopped into bite-sized chunks
- 125g (4oz) field mushrooms, quartered
- 2 cloves garlic, chopped
- 3 cups fish stock
- 455g (1lb) canned tomatoes, seeded and chopped
- 1 bay leaf
- ¼ tsp rosemary, crushed to a powder
- ¼ tsp oregano, crushed to a powder
- a pinch chili flakes
- 1 zucchini, cut into bite-sized chunks
- 1 jar standard oysters
- parsley to garnish

1. Heat oil in large saucepan and sauté the onions and mushrooms, until the onions are golden and the mushrooms are brown. Add garlic and stir for a minute. Add fish stock, chopped tomatoes and the juice reserved from the can of tomatoes. Stir in the bay leaf, rosemary, oregano, and chili flakes. Bring to a boil, then reduce heat and simmer, partially covered, for 25 minutes.
2. Add zucchini, cover and simmer for another 5 minutes, until the zucchini is almost tender. Slip the oysters with their liquid into the soup and cook, uncovered, until the edges of the oysters begin to curl. (You want them tender, not chewy.)
3. Ladle into bowls. Sprinkle with parsley and serve immediately.

Serves 4

Note: This spicy and chunky chowder is just the thing for a warming lunch or a light dinner with lots of side dishes.

Shellfish Stew

Preparation 35 mins **Cooking** approximately 30 mins **Calories** 100

- 750g (1¾lb) live lobster or 2 frozen lobster tails
- 6 tbsps olive oil
- 500g (18oz) shrimp, shelled
- 500g (18oz) fresh cod, monkfish, or other firm-fleshed fish steak
- 250g (9oz) whole small squid, cleaned
- 1 small onion, chopped
- 1 red capsicum, chopped
- 3 cloves garlic, minced
- 3 medium tomatoes, peeled, seeded and chopped
- ¼ tsp saffron thread
- 2 tbsps parsley, chopped
- 1 bay leaf
- ½ tsp dried thyme
- ¼ tsp red pepper, crushed
- ¾ cup dry white wine
- ¼ cup lemon juice
- salt and freshly ground pepper
- 12 very small clams, thoroughly scrubbed
- 12 mussels, scrubbed and de-bearded

1. As close as possible to the time you are going to cook the lobster, have the fishmonger cut the claws and tail from it and break them into serving size pieces. If using frozen lobster, cut the tails into serving size pieces.
2. Heat oil in a large, shallow, flameproof, ovenproof dish and quickly sauté lobster over high heat for 3 minutes. Remove to a platter and set aside.
3. Sauté the shrimp and fish over high heat for 1 minute and remove to platter.
4. Add squid to the dish and sauté for 1 minute. Add onion, capsicum and garlic and sauté over medium heat until onion has wilted. Stir in tomatoes, saffron, 1 tablespoon of parsley, bay leaf, thyme and crushed pepper and sauté for 2 minutes. Stir in wine, lemon juice, salt and pepper and cook, uncovered, for 10 minutes. Add reserved seafood, cover and simmer for 10 minutes longer.
5. In a covered skillet, steam clams and mussels with 2 cups of water over high heat. As clams open, remove them and add to the dish. Cut fish into pieces. Serve the stew in the dish.

Serves 6

Octopus with Potatoes and Peas

Preparation 20 mins **Cooking** approximately 1½ hrs **Calories** 125

1 kg (2¼lb) octopus, cleaned and skinned
salt
145ml (5fl oz) olive oil
1 large onion, chopped
4 garlic cloves, crushed
400g (14oz) canned tomatoes
¼ tsp ground chilies
500g (18oz) potatoes, peeled and cut into thick slices
250g (9oz) cooked peas

1 Put octopus in a large saucepan without adding water. Sprinkle with salt, cover, and let cook in its own juices over a low heat for about 45 minutes.

2 Four times during the cooking, lift the octopus out (using a fork) and dip into a pan of boiling water; then run the octopus under cold water and return it to the saucepan to continue cooking.

3 Heat olive oil in an ovenproof dish and gently fry the onion, garlic, tomatoes and chili powder for about 10 minutes (or until the onion has turned opaque). Add the potatoes and cook for about 5 minutes. Add the octopus and enough of its cooking liquid to cover the contents of the dish. Add salt as desired, and let the dish cook gently, uncovered for about 30 minutes (or until the potatoes are tender and the sauce is largely reduced).

4 Finally, add the cooked peas to the dish and heat through. Serve the octopus and vegetables straight from the dish.

Serves 4

Lobster Cheese Casserole

Preparation 10 mins **Cooking** 30 mins **Calories** 323

- 500g (18oz) lobster meat, diced
- 2 tbsps butter
- ¼ cup flour
- ¾ cup milk
- 1¼ cups heavy cream
- ½ cup shredded Cheddar cheese
- ½ tsp salt
- ¾ cup green capsicum, diced
- ¼ cup shredded Cheddar cheese
- extra pinch paprika

1 Preheat the oven to 180°C (350°F). Place the lobster in a greased 4-cup ovenproof dish. Over low heat, melt the butter, blend in the flour and slowly add the milk and cream. Cook, stirring constantly until the mixture is thick and smooth. Add the cheese, salt and capsicum. Stir until the cheese melts. Pour over the lobster. Sprinkle the extra cheese over top and garnish with the paprika. Bake in hot oven for 15 minutes. Broil for 2 minutes to brown the top and serve.

Serves 4–6

Seafood Casserole

Preparation 5 mins **Cooking** 35 mins **Calories** 228

- 1 tbsp olive oil
- 1 medium onion, roughly chopped
- 1 leek, finely chopped
- 2 cloves garlic, crushed
- 2 cups canned tomatoes
- 2 bay leaves
- 1 tbsp parsley, chopped
- ¼ cup dry white wine
- salt and freshly ground black pepper
- 1 kg (2¼lb) assorted fish and seafood
- 2 tbsps fresh oregano, chopped

1 Heat the oil in a flameproof ovenproof dish. Sauté the onion, leek and garlic until softened and slightly golden.

2 Add the tomatoes, bay leaves, parsley, wine, salt and pepper. Bring to the boil, cover and simmer gently for 20 minutes.

3 Stir in any firm-fleshed fish and simmer for 5 minutes. Stir in the soft-fleshed fish, placing the shellfish on the top.

4 Cover with a lid and continue cooking for 5–7 minutes (until the fish is tender) and the shellfish have opened (discarding any that remain closed).

5 Serve garnished with the oregano.

Serves 4–6

Note: Suitable fish and seafood include red mullet, monkfish, sea bream, cod, calamari, mussels, shelled shrimp and clams.

Baby Vegetable Curry with Pears

Preparation 20 mins **Cooking** 50 mins **Calories** 147

- 3 tbsps groundnut oil
- 2 onions, finely chopped
- 6 cloves garlic, finely chopped
- 2 pears, peeled, cored and finely chopped
- 3 tbsps tomato paste
- 2 tbsps mild curry powder
- 2 cups vegetable stock
- salt and black pepper
- 1½ cups baby carrots
- 1½ cups broccoli florets
- 1½ cups baby cauliflower, quartered
- 3 tbsps chopped cilantro leaves

1. Heat the oil in a large, heavy-based saucepan. Add the onions and garlic and fry for 6–8 minutes until golden. Add the pears and fry for a further 6–8 minutes, stirring and scraping the bottom of the pan occasionally until the pears soften and start to brown. Add a little water if the mixture becomes too dry.
2. Stir in the tomato paste and curry powder and fry for 1–2 minutes to release the flavors. Add the stock, season and bring to the boil. Reduce the heat and simmer, uncovered, for 15 minutes or until the liquid has slightly reduced.
3. Add the carrots, cover, then simmer for 5 minutes. Add the broccoli and cauliflower, cover, then simmer for a further 10–15 minutes, until the vegetables are tender. Sprinkle with the cilantro just before serving.

Serves 6

Note: Pears add a delicious sweetness to this spicy curry, which is great with basmati rice. Use a selection of ready-prepared baby vegetables to cut down on the preparation time if you like.

Braised Vegetables with a Cheddar Crust

Preparation 30 mins **Cooking** 1 hr 35 mins **Calories** 522

4 tbsps olive oil
2 tbsps butter
2 red onions, thinly sliced
1 head celery, thickly sliced
2 large carrots, thickly sliced
2 cloves garlic, crushed
salt and black pepper
4 large open mushrooms, sliced
3 red capsicums, deseeded and cut into strips
1 tsp each dried oregano and thyme
2 eggplants, thickly sliced
1 cup vegetable stock

Crust
2 cups flour
2 tsps baking powder
5 tbsps chilled butter, cubed
5 tbsps shredded Cheddar cheese
2 tbsps fresh breadcrumbs
1/2 cup heavy cream
2 tbsps chopped fresh parsley
1 tsp dried oregano

1. Heat 1 tablespoon of the oil with 1 tablespoon of butter in a large skillet. Add the onions, celery, carrots and garlic. Cook for 10 minutes, stirring often. Season, remove from the pan and set aside.
2. Preheat the oven to 200°C (400°F). Heat another tablespoon of oil in the pan, add the mushrooms, capsicums, oregano and thyme and cook for 5 minutes, stirring often. Season and add to the other vegetables. Heat the remaining oil and fry the eggplant for 3 minutes, turning once, to brown.
3. Grease an ovenproof dish with the remaining butter. Add the vegetables, pour in the stock and loosely cover with aluminum foil. Cook for 40 minutes. Remove the aluminum foil, stir and cook for a further 5 minutes or until tender.
4. Meanwhile, make the crust. Sift the flour and baking powder into a bowl. Rub in the butter, until the texture resembles coarse breadcrumbs. Mix in the Cheddar, breadcrumbs, cream, parsley and oregano and season. Increase the oven temperature to 230°C (450°F). Spoon the crust mixture over the vegetables. Cook for 20 minutes or until golden. Set aside to rest for 10 minutes before serving.

Serves 6

Note: A vegetarian entrée with a rich deep flavor that will satisfy even the most die-hard carnivores.

Index